CHAMPIONSHIP JUDO

Tai-Otoshi and O-Uchi-Gari Attacks

T. P. LEGGETT
8th Dan
(6th DAN KODOKAN)

and

KISABURO WATANABE
7th Dan

General Attacking Movement

Trevor Leggett Adhyatma Yoga Trust

Published in 2021 by
Trevor Leggett Adhyatma Yoga Trust

PO Box 362
King's Lynn
PE31 8WQ
United Kingdom

Website Address; www.tlayt.org

First published by W.Foulsham & co Ltd, London in 1964
Ippon Books edition published in 1994

ISBN: 978-1-911467-11-3

This book is dedicated to John Newman MBE, 5th Dan (1935-1993)
who demonstrated exemplary judo skills during his career which included
2nd Dan champion of Europe.
In *Championship Judo,* he was the capable uke.

CONTENTS

Foreword

The Trevor Leggett Adhyatma Yoga Trust ('TLAYT') is a registered charity established following the death of Trevor Leggett in August 2000. Its objectives are to promote the public knowledge of Yoga, Vedanta, Buddhism, Zen, Judo and Shogi.

Before his sad death in September 2019, Kisaburo Watanabe was aware of and approved the Trustees intention to republish 'Championship Judo – Taiotoshi and Ouchigari attacks' in new soft back printed and e-book editions.

The Trustees would like to thank Nicolas Soames for his kind permission to reprint his Preface, that first appeared in the Ippon Books edition of 'Championship Judo' in 1994, and for his valuable advice and his encouragement to bring out this new edition. Our thanks are also due to Tony Sweeney, Dr Michael Callan, Ben Anderson and Dave Horton-Jones for the help that they have given to us in the preparation of this edition.

The Trustees
Trevor Leggett Adhyatma Yoga Trust
February 2021

Preface

Championship Judo – Tai-Otoshi and O-Uchi-Gari Attacks by Trevor Leggett and Kisaburo Watanabe was the first judo book written in English which truly revealed the hidden riches and complexities in judo technique.

In that sense, when it was published in 1964, it proved a milestone to many who read it. Here, at last, was a comprehensible account of the careful development of a throw – *Taiotoshi* – from its very first beginnings to its full glory when, joined with a sister throw, it was ready to be executed under contest conditions.

Its clear description of crucial details – whether the grips or the standards of uchikomi which need to be attained – made it one of the very few judo books which could be usefully studied.

Like all important texts, it hasn't really dated. The photographs may not be up to modern standards but the content is as relevant now as it was 30 years ago. This, alone, means that it should remain in print.

When I first read it, I was a brown belt aspiring to a dan grade and it made an enormous difference to my personal understanding of judo.

More importantly, the effect of the book stayed with me for years, and proved to be a direct inspiration for the foundation of the Judo Masterclass series published by Ippon Books. Looking back at Tai-Otoshi and O-Uchi-Gari Attacks, I wonder whether any judo book will be able to match it for sheer clarity, purpose and understanding.

In the end, this book is a model not just for two specific throws but for all our judo training. I cannot commend it to you more highly.

Nicolas Soames
(1994)

Introduction

The main aim of this book is to introduce the reader to *general attacking Judo movement,* using as examples the throws which are centred round Taiotoshi. We are trying to convey something of the spring and dash of a good Judo attacker; for this purpose the camera strips are not a series of individually posed pictures but are stages of one and the same continuous movement.

From the very beginning it is a good thing if the student tries to imitate to some extent the free and flexible action of the expert; analysis of individual techniques tends to cramp the movement, because a beginner may think that everything has to start off from a given position in order to succeed. Whereas the truth is that successful Judo is largely dependent on being able to keep balance and control in the fast interchanges. The standard of individual technique in world Judo is getting higher; the weakness is in the general movement, and this book aims at that. We are taking mainly the Taiotoshi movement to illustrate the themes because if too many throws are described the student once again falls into the error of supposing that until every detail has been mastered nothing can be done, and the student also tends to suppose that for each position there is one appropriate throw.

This is quite a common delusion in Judo. Either Judo students fancy they have to learn a number of throws corresponding to a number of 'weaknesses' in the opponent's position or movement, or else they think they will learn one throw well, and just wait till the appropriate opportunity presents itself. As a matter of fact the basic technique of a throw is only the beginning of

1

mastery; no Judo student has reached expert level at a throw till he knows how to manoeuvre the opponent into it, and till furthermore he can execute it from all sorts of unorthodox attitudes. Before reading further, try the 'flicker' at the top right corners of pages 79 to 27 of this book; the attacker is carried right up into the air, but manages to control his opponent's throw, and comes shooting down into his Taiotoshi. This is the kind of Judo which must be developed, and this is the spirit of attack.

Judo students, from the beginning, must get spring into their movements. Have a look at the section called 'Tricks of Holding' and notice how the man rises on tiptoe and sinks right down, then rises again and sinks again, to come up for the last time as he executes the throw. Exercise yourself in thus *changing the level* in your Judo; if you look through the pictures in this book with this one point in mind, you will have learnt something very useful. Many Europeans hate bending their knees to go down; they would rather keep the knees straight and bend forward to pick something up than bend the knees and go down. Well, in Judo you have to train yourself to bend the knees flexibly and naturally, and at speed. Some experts do a hundred or two 'squats' every morning and evening to help them acquire the movement comfortably.

Again study the *change of distance* in the various attacks; it is no use keeping the same distance from your opponents and hoping they will somehow walk into your throw; you have to chase after them and cover the ground faster than they can. There is a Zen story about a man who was walking in a field one day when he saw a rabbit pop out of its hole suddenly and stun itself against a stake which the farmer had happened to fix there. He took the rabbit home and had it for dinner. Afterwards he used to sit there for hours every day waiting for the same thing to happen again. But it never did. Some Judo students are a bit like this; when they are beginners they manage to get hold of a technique which works when the opponent happens to come right into it. But as they get on they meet better opponents, and then the opponent never walks into the throw again.

We have chosen Taiotoshi to illustrate these principles of movement because it is a throw where the whole body is moved, and where the principle of the throw is not confused by hooking, reaping or sweeping movements of one leg as in many other throws. If you learn the actions of going in to the opponent, chasing, circling, and tricking and so on with this throw, you can apply them to most other throws without more than minor changes in technique.

We are using 'I' and 'You' in this book because it is intended as a straightforward training manual. The technical words are Tori (for the attacker) and Uke (for the one thrown). The other technical words mainly explain themselves: you can see a picture of Taiotoshi on the front cover and in hundreds of places in the book; Ouchi (short for Ouchigari) you can see in the section called The 'Y'; Kosotogari similarly you will see in Section 21.

The demonstrations in this book are almost all performed by K. Watanabe; no-one can be equally skilled in all Judo movement, but the techniques are mostly his. The pictures are taken from actual practice at full speed (except for a few such as the right-hand slip pictures where the action is not normally clearly visible and which have been posed) with a new camera specially designed for analysis of sports movement. We made a great number of pictures and then selected those where the point to be illustrated appeared from a favourable angle. It is hoped that a realistic effect has been achieved which will give a good notion of movement.

We are grateful to Mr. John Newman, teacher at the Renshuden Judo Club, for making a more vigorous and determined opponent than the lay figure of so many Judo books; thanks also go to Mr. T. Kawamura for the pictures in Section 21, and to Mr. George Kerr, teacher at the Renshuden, and to the members of the Club for help and suggestions.

THE AUTHORS
(1964)

1. How to Build Up Attacking Movement

One purpose of this book is to explain how to build up attacks on Taiotoshi and its main partner Ouchigari, but you can use the method in learning how to master any main throw. Read the whole book quickly once, and then repeatedly run through the flicker at the top right from page 79 backwards to page 27. Then you should have a rough idea of Taiotoshi and Ouchi, and of the spirit of Judo movement.

Your Judo progress depends on three main things : *free* practice (and contest); *formal* practice of the movements; *study*. Get first a rough idea of the movement and keep trying it vigorously and enterprisingly in free practice; don't fuss too much with detail at this stage. Taiotoshi is called in Japan a 'choshi-waza', which means that timing and rhythm are all-important. One day your opponent will go down when you hardly realize you have thrown him, and this will give you an idea of what the throw really is. Study is to help you understand the principles of the throw; formal practice is to help you to begin to 'feel' the movement.

After a week or so splashing around with the rough idea, begin your study. Take one point and try to get it fairly accurate; to do this you will have to go fairly slowly, but remember it must still be a Judo movement. If you go too slow your movement will cease to be effective, even against a static opponent.

Don't expect to get the proper movement right away. Some people hope for the impossible. If you could see the body images in your brain by which you feel position and initiate movement, you would find that while an enormous number of brain-cells are devoted to fine discrimination of the hand for instance, there are comparatively very few for trunk and neck. This means that you simply cannot feel accurately your trunk posture and vary it as you want. For some time your training is in effect establishing new discriminations and control in the body images. As you try free and formal practice, the defective parts of the body images are developing. An ordinary student, for example, takes about one year before being able to stand on one leg for five minutes; in Judo you have to balance on one leg while performing difficult techniques. It takes time, but to develop good feeling and control of the body is of great value in life, and according to the Zen Buddhists, it is of importance in spiritual development as well.

Similarly, most people are hampered at first by a sort of physical timidity, a reluctance to throw themselves into a movement. This too is overcome by practice, and to solve this problem is also a great help in life. Dr. Kano, the founder of Judo, stated clearly that a real understanding of Judo principles can be applied to life as a whole, and when it is so applied, it produces a harmonious development of body, mind and character.

2. Basic Analysis of Taiotoshi

To bring out the movements clearly, a cord has been laid down with another crossing it at right angles. My opponent stands with his toe-tips just touching the cord, the feet perhaps a little wider than shoulder-width. I was standing facing him in the same position, and now, in Fig. 1, I make the first move.

First Movement. I step on to the cross with my right foot. Make the step with the toes; if the foot comes flat on the mats, the large area will increase friction and I shall not be able to turn smoothly later on.

The pulling hand is the left, and the little-finger edge of it should turn outwards. I should feel that I am pulling along the outer edge of my arm. This is an important point to which I shall return again and again.

Second Movement. Fig. 2 shows my left foot coming into position, the toes on one cord and the heel on the other, making a little triangle with the cords (this will be explained in detail later).

Figs. 2–4 show the right-hand action. From the beginning I must try to bring in my right hand, which means doubling up the elbow as much as I can. We all know how it is difficult to hold a weight at arm's-length where it is easy if you hold it close to you, and the principle here is the same.

Beginners get so excited in the early stages that they tighten and stiffen the right shoulder and elbow; the result is that their right hand gives the

FIG. 1   FIG. 2   FIG 3

FIG. 4   FIG. 5   FIG. 6

opponent a sort of poke which actually forces him away instead of drawing him in.

In Fig. 3 the right leg prepares to come in. Beginners also tend in their excitement to make this leg hard, and almost to kick out with it. Practise this movement, keeping the leg very soft.

In Fig. 4 the right leg shoots into position. I should not try to bring it tightly against the opponent's leg, but perhaps two inches away. Notice that my right foot crosses the cord.

Third Movement (Figs. 5–8). The vital thing is to throw all the weight on to the hands. From a subconscious fear of falling, beginners hold back; they should practise using a chair, if necessary, to get the feel of it. See the section on Throwing the Weight in Taiotoshi.

Fig. 6 shows how low the knee goes. If it gets right down, it is easier for my pull to bring his shin on top of the leg.

In Fig. 8 I begin the springing-up action. I have got the opponent bending right over, and in fact I bear him up with the back of my right leg.

Fourth Movement. This is the actual execution of the throw, and needs no special explanation here – if the preceding movements are done well, it will come off by itself. Beginners on the contrary are in such a hurry to get on to this part that they leave out the previous moves and try to make up for everything with one big heave at the end. Such Judo always leads to failure, unless you are much stronger than your opponent, and even then it often does not score.

Now that you have had a look at the pictures and been told the main points, try it out roughly with an opponent. Don't bother too much about getting all the points right; get the general movement first, say about twenty times. Then let your opponent try twenty times, and have a good look at what he is doing. It will help you to see what is wrong with your own attempts.

Don't try to go too fast for your balance. On the other hand, don't go so slowly that you stagger while transferring your weight. You can walk fast and you can walk slowly, but there comes a point when to go any slower means that you are no longer doing the same thing at all; the pace is no longer even and the movements have to be completely artificial.

FIG. 7

FIG. 8

FIG. 9

FIG. 10

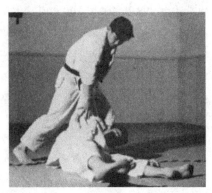

FIG. 11

It's the same in Judo movement; you should at the beginning take it very comfortably, but if you go too slow you find you are not comfortable.

When you have done the first round of twenty, do another round but taking up one of the points, such as the left arm pull. Never mind about the rest of the movement, whether it's right or wrong, but get your left arm and shoulder working loose, moving more and more freely and going higher and more out. You will begin to get the *feel* of what it is like to make a very full wide pull. When you begin to get that feel, you can allow yourself to speed up naturally, bit by bit. But once you find that you've begun to skimp your pull, that you are just jerking briefly because you can't find time to fit in the long pull, then reduce the speed until you can get it in.

Don't expect to get everything right straight away, and don't feel you must get one thing perfect before you move on to the next. People will tell you that if you are 'practising it wrong' you can't improve. They imply that if you make mistakes at the beginning you will get worse and worse. Well, think of beginners learning to ride a bicycle. They keep falling off, but no one would accuse them of 'practising it wrong'. They are feeling for a particular thing, the sense of balance, and they can't expect to get it at once. In the same way in Judo you are feeling for the balance and rhythm of the throw, and you won't get it for a good time. The instructions and analysis are to get your movement somewhat along the right lines; when you are doing something like it, one day you will find the opponent suddenly seems light and goes over with unexpected ease. Now that's the first flash – and you should note very carefully how you 'felt' when it happened. All the descriptions and suggestions are only to get you to this point, and to bring you back to it when you lose it, as will happen again and again.

Uke can help. He should never give way like a reed in the wind, but hold himself firmly. At first he should not take any active counter-measures, but as you progress in the throw, after say about three months, your Ukes should brace their hips strongly so that you get the idea of hitting against something. Then your throws come in repeatedly like a succession of waves against a rock, and with something of that rhythm. This is for the static repetitions; the moving Uchikomi repetitions will be described later on.

11

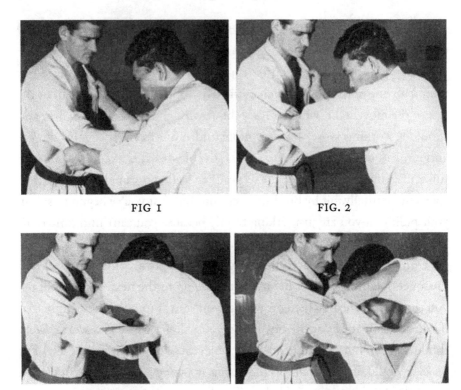

FIG I

FIG. 2

FIG. 3

FIG. 4

FIG 5

3. The Left-hand Pull

Pictures 1–5 show an ideal left-arm pull; the little-finger edge of the hand is turned right out and even up, and the elbow is carried well up and away.

The grip is taken with the small fingers; don't try to hold mainly with the thumb and big fingers pinching the jacket, but instead twine the cloth round the small fingers. Through practising this method of pulling (it comes in many other throws as well) the muscle on the outer edge of the palm becomes developed – you can see the bulge in some of these pictures. Fig. 5 also shows the muscles along the outer edge of the arm coming into action. The feeling is of pulling from the little finger, along the outside edge of the arm and shoulder, and so down the left side. I cannot describe the feeling better than this; I recommend all aspiring Taiotoshi experts to try to reproduce it in their Uchikomi and practice.

You will notice that my left-hand hold is on the outside of the sleeve. It *is* possible to have your arm underneath his, gripping the lapel or near it, or to do the same when holding over his arm. But very few of the Taiotoshi experts hold anywhere except the sleeve, and I believe that to try to develop a major Taiotoshi from a lapel grip is to begin at a disadvantage. Of course, as a strategic surprise move, such a Taiotoshi will come off admirably sometimes, but this is just because you do not try it often and so can take the opponent completely aback.

Theoretically the lapel hold means a lessening of the distance between the two bodies; where you want to come tightly against the opponent, as in many Koshi-waza, to begin from a near position may be a help. But in Taiotoshi you do not come against him, and if you begin with a grip on the lapel, you will often find that his arms are very effective in defence against your body. Whereas if you look at Figs. 3–5 you will see that any push with his right arm only helps my own pull and turn.

Practise this movement till your arm is tired; combine it with the step in, but let this last be very approximate for the time being. Try to get the feel of throwing your arm up and out, and the opponent's arm with it. *Don't skimp the big curve out in the interests of speed;* build up speed later.

4. Foot Position

Dabblers in Taiotoshi often enter as in Figs. 1–3. The idea is that the left foot, the supporting one, should be well outside the opponent's left foot, so as not to be in front of him. It is thought that if the thrower is in front of the opponent, he will find his own body in the way when the time comes to make the throw.

This kind of Taiotoshi aims at throwing the opponent straight forward, and it assumes either:

(i)   that opponent's weight is equally distributed on his two feet, in which case his weakness is at right angles to the line joining his two big toes; or

(ii) that he can be tricked into leaning or rushing straight forward.

Now I don't deny that these things can be brought about, and very spectacularly sometimes. When I say this is the Taiotoshi of a 'dabbler' I mean that it is the Taiotoshi of someone whose main throw is something else and who just slips in a Taiotoshi if the chance exceptionally occurs; this method cannot be made the basis of Taiotoshi as a main throw.

A theoretical criticism of the relative position of the feet in Fig. 3 is that we end up with the four feet roughly along the same line, so that the line of strength (across) and the line of weakness (forward) become the same for both. Then, as thrower, I have no advantage of position, and the throw will not be easy. A practical criticism is that contest experience shows that Tori,

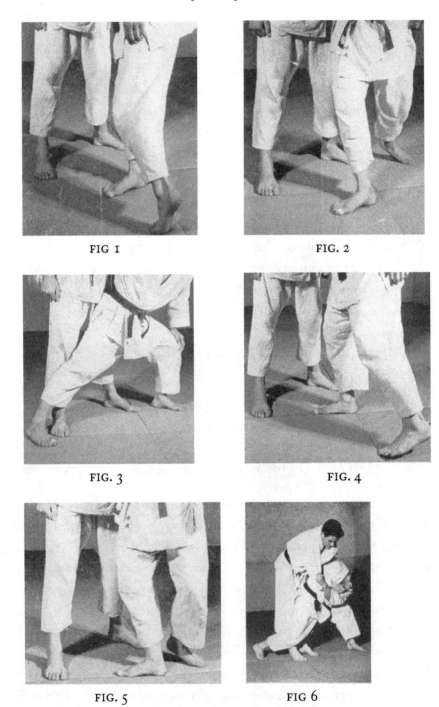

FIG 1

FIG. 2

FIG. 3

FIG. 4

FIG. 5

FIG 6

the thrower, frequently gets pulled over backwards, a direction in which he is weak.

Therefore I generally recommend a basic Taiotoshi not to the opponent's front but more to his right-front, which is an opportunity that comes up much more frequently; if you look at Figs. 4 and 5 you will see how the feet should go. (Plot them out against the lines of the mats, as explained in the Basic section, pages 7-11.) Notice that it will be much harder for an opponent to pull me over backwards because I am not so close to his left foot.

Fig. 6, which was not posed but taken from practice, shows how the throw develops. My body is a bit in front of his, but if I get low I do not get in his way but instead my body weight helps to pull him down; further, as I am throwing to his right-front (and not to his front) I can afford to be a bit in front of his left side without impeding the throw.

I believe this form of Taiotoshi is the one to study first; when you get expert at it you can bring off other forms as the special circumstances arise. But this is the safest and strongest one in contest.

Practise this foot movement till you can do it lightly and dexterously; at the beginning just hold on with the left hand and combine the long, wide pull with your foot movement. Keep your body and legs soft and drop down well towards the end, in readiness for the spring.

FIG. 3

FIG. 2

FIG. 1

FIG. 4

FIG. 7

FIG. 5

FIG. 6

5. Circling Uchikomi

One generally thinks of Uchikomi as practice of repetition with the opponent standing still. This is the fundamental way of doing it, but I believe that 'moving' Uchikomi is very important for getting free movement in Randori and that it should be brought to the fore. (In the old days there was a type of Randori in which you were expected to attempt a given throw forty or fifty times in quick succession, but this has dropped into disuse.)

The sequence of circling Taiotoshi practice as shown here is for Taiotoshi from the Right Shizentai position. Tori is the thrower or attacker, and Uke makes a moving defence. (Follow the pictures around in a circle.)

The principle is that Uke prepares to jump or step over Tori's right leg as it makes the attack. You can see in the first few pictures how Uke has jumped across as Tori throws himself in. Uke anticipates the throw just as in contest, by bringing his left foot up to his right foot so that he can make his step or jump more easily; you can see this in the very first picture. (Notice that this means Tori's left foot comes outside Uke's left foot, which is not what was explained in the basic Taiotoshi; the reason is that here Uke has shifted his left foot from its original position in order to make his jump.)

The first sequence is 1–3. In the flurry the feet are very far apart and so the weight has come on to the heel of the left foot. You have to get used to these unusual positions and learn how to recover balance and posture quickly. In this connection see the contest picture of Mr. Hashimoto (7th

19

Dan) in which too the feet are very far apart, but in spite of it he managed to bring off the throw.

In Fig. 4 Tori comes shooting in again and this time goes in very low; Uke just has time to step over and then has to jump clear as Tori springs up from below (Figs. 5–7). Without waiting to pause or recover balance, Tori comes in straight away for the next one (Fig. 1 again).

These pictures were taken from actual practice; don't look for details in them, but try to get from the general outline how Tori runs after Uke and throws himself in. Most people feel they have to recover balance after making one attempt; they want to start with a clean sheet as it were, because they feel if they begin the attack with uncertain balance they cannot make the throw well. What they forget is that while they are getting back their balance, the opponent is getting back his too. The whole point of this Uchikomi is to train you to get control and feeling even in positions which are very rapidly changing; it's true that your throw will not be so powerful, but your opponent will be much weaker. The ideal of Judo is not to smash through an opponent's strongest point but to get him off balance and keep him off balance; then even if your attack has some defects it will often suffice to get him over. And this is the real principle of Judo; not to overcome the opponent by overwhelming force against his strong point, but to overcome him with much less force by applying it against his weak point. When I say 'less force' I do not mean you should hold back; but I mean that the emphasis is on speed and 'mixing it', and not on planting yourself firmly like a weight-lifter has to do before he makes his lift.

6. The Right Hand

Some Judo opponents seem to be rocks; you pull and pull and it is like coming against a wall. But, in fact, they are not rocks. Often such a one is physically not specially strong, but he knows how to use his muscles and weight, and is two or three times more effective than the ordinary opponent. You have to learn how to neutralize a skilful Judo defence. It is the function of your right hand to offset a left-hand defence by your opponent, which is one of the main methods of stopping Taiotoshi (and many of the hip throws also).

In the main line of pictures (Figs. 1–9) you will see the action of my right hand when it is holding *underneath*. We have released the hold with the other hand in order that the movement may be clearly visible. As a matter of fact in ordinary practice this action is not easy to see, and perhaps for that reason it is not widely mastered.

In Figs. 1–3 I have an opponent who uses an arm like an iron bar against my chest. When I try to come in, he thrusts at me and forces me out. The first thing is for me to pull so that momentarily he thrusts even more strongly.

Now my idea is to loosen his Judogi. In Fig. 5 you can see how I pull it out with just a finger grip until I get it fairly near my chest. I am twisting my chest to the right so that his thrusting right arm begins to slide past. My right elbow should be tight against my body, and I must bring the right hand fully against my chest before I try to slide him off (Fig. 7). His arm comes off when my hand is against my chest, and then I slide my chest forward past his hand, which has been made to slide off by a slight pressure from inside from my hand (Fig. 8).

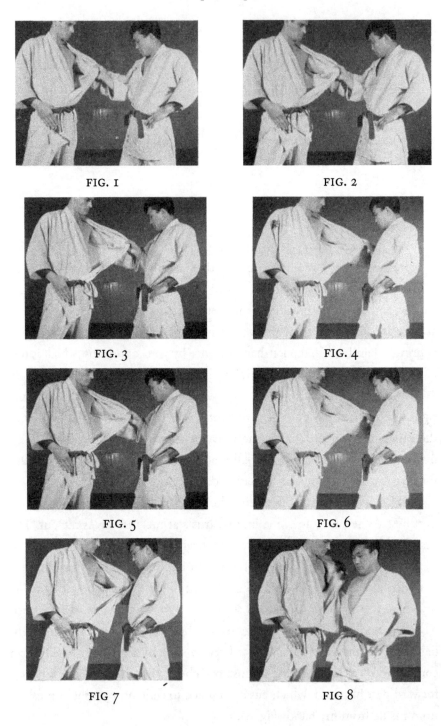

FIG. 1

FIG. 2

FIG. 3

FIG. 4

FIG. 5

FIG. 6

FIG 7

FIG 8

Fig. 9 shows the turn of the whole body, with the opponent being fished up on the slack of the Judogi gathered up on the right hand.

FIG. 9

FIG 10

FIG 11

I. – *The Slip*

The first part of the movement is the same as in Figs. 1–4 of the previous section. Then, instead of pulling as in Fig. 5, I must twist my hand so that the back presses his arm out. Then I thrust so as to take his Judogi out. The most important thing is the use of the back of the hand on the opponent's arm and then out. If I get this well, the Judogi will almost come off his shoulder, and it will slide right off mine. Now he can no longer use his arm to block my coming in. The movement is shown in Figs. 10 and 11. (They are taken from the rear to show it clearly.)

23

Once I have got his arm off I must snatch my arm back into the position of Fig. 9.

If I make this movement too lazily, he can sometimes trap my arm by pressing his body down on to it, so I must be extremely lively with my snatching back action.

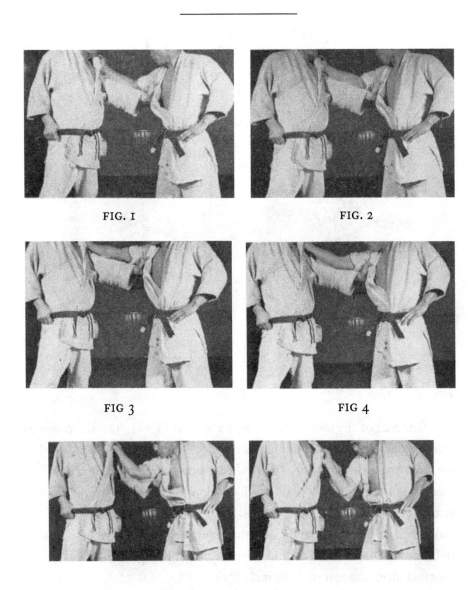

FIG. I   FIG. 2

FIG 3   FIG 4

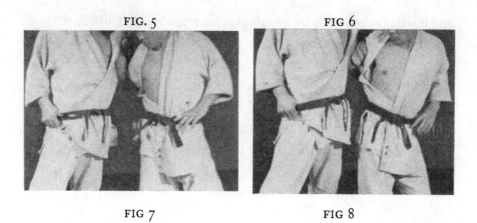

FIG. 5   FIG 6

FIG 7   FIG 8

II. – *The Slip from on Top*

In the scuffles and mock wrestling matches which children have everywhere, they often try to catch round the waist and swing the other one over. Children usually try to get the under-grip. In our sport called Sumo, which is very popular in Japan, the amateur wrestlers also generally try to hold underneath, but it is a fact that the strongest champions deliberately permit the opponent to take the under-grip and themselves take the upper one. In Judo, too, children and beginners seek to get the underneath hold, but the most skilful ones often specialize in an upper hold. Even very small and light Judoka, such as Iwata (10 st. 6 lb.) who was finalist in the Judo tournament of the Asian Games when it was held in Tokyo, Asahi (6th Dan) and recently Yoshigaki (4th Dan), all get repeated successes with the upper grip. However, it is necessary to know the techniques for overcoming the opponent's resistance.

You can easily see the method from the photographs (Figs. 1–8). The main point, which is not so obvious, is that I should try to get the elbow across as far from the opponent's shoulder as possible. It is easier to bring it over much higher up, near his shoulder, but then it is not very effective, and it is harder to follow up by bringing my chest in and doubling the right elbow to the fullest extent.

As with the previous slip, you should effect it well down Tori's stiff arm, when it will have more leverage and will be harder for him to avoid.

The right arm should be loose; I think that foreigners tend to keep their arms too rigid and try to force their throws unreasonably. If they try to master some of these neat little tricks, their Judo will become much more effective.

7. Comparisons

Have a look at these four pictures of the preliminary step; they show how to hang on the other man with your weight and pull him forward as you pull yourself in. There is nothing heavy about this movement; it is like a bounce or spring.

Now here are four pictures of the turn; you can see how much variation there can be in the action even when executed by the same man. Yet the main points – especially the upward pulling left arm, are substantially the same. Note the lightness and energy of the movement; it must be like a dancing step.

Lastly, here are pictures of the throwing action, in two cases successful and in two cases where the opponent is jumping over. Notice the way the head is thrown into the throwing action. These pictures were all taken from an actual fast Randori.

8. Uchikomi with a Pillar

With what you have studied so far, you should begin serious and lively Uchikomi or repetition practice. This means coming in and out in a rhythm, thinking at first of one single point and trying to get that right, and when you have approximated to it, just coming in and out and feeling for the position.

In the West it is quite hard to find a good Uke or opponent for Uchikomi. Most of them, from a mistaken idea of 'co-operation' simply give way before the pull comes in at all. That means you get no idea of the feel of the throw in practice. So here you are using a bicycle inner tube, put round a pillar; that will give you almost the same feel as a good Uke, who stands holding himself braced against your throw. The 'give' in the inner tube is about equivalent to the elasticity and spring in the body of a good Uke; there is a slight give as you come in and then he becomes firm so that you can throw your weight in.

Figs. 1–10 show the throw on the right, and then Figs. 11–19 show it on the left; you should aim to do about the same number each side. Your way of executing the throw to right and left will never be quite the same, because your body to begin with is not quite symmetrical, but it will develop freedom of movement and give you some new ideas if you practise both sides.

FIG. 1   FIG. 2   FIG. 3   FIG. 4

FIG. 5   FIG. 6   FIG. 7   FIG. 8

FIG. 9   FIG. 10   FIG. 11   FIG 12

FIG. 13   FIG. 14   FIG. 15   FIG. 16

FIG. 17   FIG 18   FIG. 19

When coming in I try to see that my head keeps in line with the pillar; that means my weight a good deal on the leading foot. If my weight falls on to the rear foot, in other words if I fall away, I shall tend to lose balance and collapse backwards.

The head weight is a big proportion of the whole body weight, and its handling is important. I try to look hard at the pillar about the height of my eyes, while coming in. Then I can keep straight. It's like a man walking – if he keeps his eyes on the ground he tends to lose direction. In Niigata, where I was born and spent my childhood, there are heavy snowfalls in the winter because it is in the north of Japan. I remember when we were children we used to try to see who could walk the straightest over a fresh untrodden space of snow. I found out then that you have to keep your eyes fixed rigidly on some point straight ahead. If you look down even for a moment, then afterwards when you examine the line of steps, you find it wavered at that point (K.W.).

Now on the movement itself, and taking the right side movement as the example. My feeling is that the first movement is the short pull (i.e. with the right hand – the one whose shoulder is coming in). The second is the long pull out with the left hand, feeling the pull along the outside edge of the hand, arm shoulder and body as I have explained previously; third comes the feeling of the band across my elbow or somewhere near it (see Fig. 13). Sometimes the band comes across the shoulder, but that is more like the practice for Seoinage, and I should try to feel it across the elbow as much as I can.

The 'short pull' hand should be straight as possible at the wrist.

The hips don't touch the pillar, but drop down just before contact is made. I try to get as close as possible to the pillar without actually touching.

The starting distance is about twice my arm's length from the pillar. I sometimes try more – for instance, I stand sideways on with the finger-tips of one stretched arm against the pillar, and then stretch the other arm out to the other side; I see where the fingers come above the mat, and stand there. This gives me a distance of both arms and the body width to cover. The extra distance is not so easy at the beginning, but to practise it comes in very useful later on, because in contest you sometimes have to cover a good deal of ground very quickly and boldly.

The pictures will give an idea of the movement; remember you have to go out with as much spring and elasticity as you came in; don't collapse and flop once you have completed the 'throwing' action, but keep your body full of energy. You need not put tremendous strength into these movements, but you must keep your body full of liveliness.

Timing: a beginner should expect to cover about 30 repetitions in a minute.

Gradually increase your speed without losing the full sweep of the movement, and without shortening the distance you cover, till you get somewhere near 40–50 repetitions, a fair number for someone approaching Black Belt standard.

An expert should get in about 50–60 a minute.

FIG. I

FIG. 2

FIG. 3

FIG. 4

FIG 5

FIG. 6

FIG 7

9. Throwing the Weight in Taiotoshi

Fig. 1 shows the feel of the weight in Taiotoshi. It is a good thing to try it once or twice with a chair every evening for a week or so; somehow people are willing to throw their weight on to a chair, but reluctant when it is an opponent.

Of course the chair is in front of me, whereas in Taiotoshi the opponent is at first behind, but if you look at Figs. 2–4 you will understand. The weight has to be thrown forward as the opponent comes over. As he passes over the top, my own body will be pulled back on to balance again in most cases (though admittedly in high-grade contests we often deliberately go to the ground with the opponent to make sure of getting him pinned to the mats).

In Figs. 5, 6 and 7 I am going as fast as I can; if you look carefully at the blur at the bottom of Fig. 5, you will see that my near foot is off the ground and the far foot is on tiptoe; this means I am throwing myself at him (notice also the raised elbow). In Fig. 6, I am getting in and dropping down, my whole weight hanging on to him; in Fig. 7 he has gone over in a big whirl and my body has come upright with the reaction. The return to balance is nothing conscious; his weight does it for me and I don't need to think anything about it.

A big factor in throwing the weight into the throw is the handling of the *head*. The chin should be drawn in as much as you can – some teachers tell you to bring it into the hollow below the Adam's apple, others tell you to try to trap your left lapel with it at the moment when you execute the throwing action. You will get the notion from Figs. 2, 3 and 4; in Figs. 5 and 6 you can see how the head is thrown in. In fact, it has been done energetically so that the hair has come forward, and if you like you can try whether you can get your own hair to come out over your eyes like this!

FIG. I

FIG. 2

FIG 3

FIG 4

FIG. 5

FIG. 6

10. Different Points of Contact

In Fig. 1 the hip is very far through; many theorists would classify this throw as a Tsuri-komi-goshi or even a Seoi-nage.

Similarly, in Fig. 2, the hip is actually against the opponent and it might be classified as a hip throw. However, the whole movement is based on the Taiotoshi action, and this is one of the many cases where Judo throws shade into each other. The deciding point should be whether, in fact, the throw is made by the weight of the body transmitted through the hands, or whether the contact of the hips is an essential factor of the throw.

In Fig. 3 the top part of the leg is making contact, and in Fig. 4 there is no contact at all because the opponent has succeeded in disengaging his right leg. However, the throw is so well on that in fact the opponent was brought over; he was not able to get his right foot over in time to support himself (Fig. 5).

In general, it is better to have a shallow contact than to get too far through; in the latter case, the whole throw can easily collapse (Fig. 6).

A special thing to notice in these pictures of the contact moment is how my *head* has been thrown forward; in some of the pictures you can see how the hair has flopped out because the head was moved energetically.

The management of the head is tremendously important in Taiotoshi, as in nearly all other throws; ideally the chin should come down on top of the left lapel or somewhere near it. We cannot always achieve a perfect head position, but it is a point to be checked on periodically, especially during stale periods.

Akio Kaminaga, three times All-Japan champion, and a specialist in left-hand Taiotoshi. The throw is only partly successful here because the opponent has managed to avoid being pinned on to his left foot. The thrower could not get his own weight on to his own pulling hand (the right), and gives the other man some play. Taiotoshi frequently fails in this way. (In the contest, Kaminaga stumbled his opponent and won on the ground.)

11. The Chase

In Judo you must get the spirit of the chase; it is the only way in which you can beat someone bigger and stronger than yourself. Have a look first at this set of seven pictures, taken from an actual Randori. In the first one the man has just jumped over a Taiotoshi, but the pull has whirled him well round. Then he must be pursued, without giving him any rest in which to recover his physical and especially mental balance. Look at the attacker's posture in the second picture and you will get an idea of how to keep up the tension.

In Fig. 3 he has thrown himself in again at the man who this time only gets out by jumping right over (you can see his feet in mid-air in Fig. 4). Now *this* is the moment! Very many British Judo students can get to this point, when they get a near-miss. But then they stop to get themselves ready for a fresh attack, and so the opportunity goes, because the opponent also settles himself firmly, this time fortified with the knowledge that he has survived one Taiotoshi, and with the 'feel' of it in his body.

It is just when the opponent has made a desperate recovery that your best chance comes. Of course, probably your own balance is not good, but that may not matter too much; if you can make any sort of attack at this moment, it often comes off. Have a good look at Fig. 4; you have to practise yourself in 'mixing it' in such situations. You must determine to go on until either you throw your opponent or you fall over yourself.

So, in Fig. 5, the attack goes on. As you can see it is not perfectly executed, but because the opponent is so unstable he finds he has to take a step forward, and that brings him right into the throw. The story does not always have this happy ending, but remember that every time you try you are building up your sense of balance for the big flurries; the real difference between the top exponents is not so much their individual techniques but how well they can keep their balance and movement in these sustained rushes.

FIG. I

FIG. 2

FIG. 3

FIG. 4

FIG. 5   FIG. 6

FIG 7

FIG. 1   FIG. 2   FIG. 3

FIG. 4   FIG. 5   FIG. 6   FIG. 7

FIG. 8   FIG. 9   FIG. 10

FIG. 11

12. The Sukashi Counter to Uchimata

This is the most important single application of Taiotoshi for the general Judo student, especially the small student. Every light Judo student must study this counter, whether he specializes in Taiotoshi or not. Note that the important one is the left Taiotoshi, because this is the counter to the right Uchimata throw. If you are small and you do not know this, a big student specializing in Uchimata (and nearly all big students do go in for this throw) will sooner or later simply pick you up with it. No small student can expect to be able to resist directly a sequence of well-directed Uchimata attacks; one of them is bound to get through, and then the weight tells. In any case it is quite wrong for the light student to attempt direct resistance, their *forte* is speed in changing their direction of movement, and they must try to develop that.

Uchimata-sukashi, or the 'Uchimata slip' is a perfect example of Judo for the small student. The body must be kept supple, or it cannot be done. The Uchimata must be anticipated, but this is not too difficult as a rule; very few big opponents can launch it without getting up steam, so to say. But sometimes, though anticipated, it cannot be stopped, and pictures 5, 6 and 7 of this series should be carefully studied.

One of the problems is that to make the counter you have to be able to slip your left leg behind your right so that your opponent's leg sweeps only the air. This normally implies that you have to stand with your whole weight on your right foot, and then what happens is that you find it difficult to come across as in Figs. 8 and 9 for the final counter.

One of the methods of solving the problem is shown here very clearly. Have a good look at the head. As the thrower comes in, you take your head to the left. In Figs. 5 and 6 on page 42 you can see that the weight of the lower part of the body is being taken by the right foot as the left leg prepares to move, but the weight of the head and upper part of the body *momentarily rests on the opponent.* This would bring you right into the throw but for the fact that you have curved your body away and got the left leg loose.

The hips must be kept soft and supple for this one; practise it in Uchi-komi with the opponent really trying the throw. You will find you can exe-cute the first part of the movement, the avoiding movement, after only a little practice, but you will generally find you have stiffened up somewhere along the line and cannot shoot in for the final Taiotoshi. You discover that you can help to keep out of the throw by push-ing with the left hand, but if you rely too much on this, forgetting the body curve, your defence becomes mainly static and you cannot follow up.

FIG. I

FIG. 2   FIG. 3

44

Have a look at the three pictures opposite on page 44. This shows the method of using the arm-thrust, but the important point is to keep the legs and hips mobile. As you can see, at the end in Fig. 3, the man on the right is in an excellent position to jump in for Taiotoshi. One of the great failings of many Judo students, even strong ones, is that they lack general mobility, and so cannot take this sort of chance. In such a case they are quite content merely to block the opponent's attack with the arm-thrust, and allow him to recover. They don't venture a sudden attack from this sort of position because they have not trained themselves to do so. When the position relative to the opponent is unusual, as it is here, they feel uncertain of themselves and have no confidence. They forget that though their own position may be relatively unstable, the opponent's is much more so. The real training is to keep balance and control in the mixed-up positions; if you can have confidence only when you have engaged with the opponent in one of the regular Shizentai positions your Judo is still very restricted. Resist the temptation to freeze hard when you are attacked, and try to get the hang of how to move out and round; you will get thrown a good deal at first, but afterwards you will get a good many unexpected successes.

FIG. 1   FIG 2   FIG 3   FIG. 4

FIG. 5   FIG. 6   FIG 7

FIG 8   FIG. 9   FIG. 10

FIG. 11   FIG. 12   FIG. 13   FIG. 14

13. Tricks of Holding

Watching Judo contests in the West, one gets the impression often that the contestants have agreed first to take up an orthodox hold and an orthodox stance. Perhaps this is a weakness in Japan too at the present.

The present series shows something more lively. My opponent has longer arms than I have myself. As he is about to take hold with his right hand, I sink a bit; this is to throw him out in his calculation of level. At the same time I push at his right hand with my left. This means he has to make a sort of lunge to get his grip (Fig. 4) and that's the first stage in my attempt to get him flustered.

Now, as I try to take hold with my left, he pushes me off with his longer arm; in Fig. 5 you can see that I have come on to tiptoe and even so I cannot reach his right lapel. So I come across for it with my right hand, and he twists away his body to take both lapels farther from me.

Still, he cannot stop my *right* shoulder coming forward (this is an important principle of Judo; when one part of the body is held, don't try to force it through, but use another part which is free), and so I grab the lapel with my right hand, and in the same movement pass it across to my left hand. An experienced contest man takes this sort of thing in his stride, but you do not often see it over here. Have a look at the contest picture of Mr. Inokuma (page 77) for an illustration from top-rank contest practice in Japan.

As I get hold with my left I slide the elbow over his arm and press down; this tends to slide his right arm out of the battle, and makes it imperative for him to hold quickly with his left (Fig. 8) so he, as a tall man, comes over the top to get his grip (Fig. 9). As he is about to take hold I, in turn, move my shoulder away (Fig. 10) to make him stretch out, and then suddenly sink and push his hand away from the inside (Fig. 11). As he clutches and clutches, I drop right down (Fig. 12) so that he bends forward in his anxiety to secure his hold quickly. I can secure my own hold from the inside and underneath, and with it I come shooting up and turn round (Fig. 13).

Then I abruptly drop right down again into Taiotoshi. He has only now got his grip and he is right in the throw.

I am not saying all these movements can be learnt by heart, but this is the *sort of thing* you should train yourself in. Train yourself in changing the level: here I was on tiptoe, then right down, then up again for the turn round, and then right down again for the throw. Again train yourself in changing the distance from the opponent, sometimes by twisting the body. Both my opponent and myself were doing this at the beginning and in the middle, to throw out the other man's calculations; if you are not quite where he expects you to be, he nearly always loses balance a little, and before he can adjust, you have a chance.

14. Jumping Taiotoshi as a Counter

This technique I (K.W.) learned from a senior at Chuo University, Mr. Okada, who when he was 4th Dan was one of our best contest men. He was 5 ft. 4 in. and weighed some 10 st. In contest he used to be carried up in the air and we Chuo supporters shut our eyes thinking it was all over – but he had jumped in anticipation and wriggled out of the throw in mid-air, coming down into position for Taiotoshi. Here are the main positions in the sequence – to see the whole thing in movement look at the flicker on the corner of pages 79-27 of this book. Hold the book in the left hand and flick the pages down, looking at the corner, and you will see the Taiotoshi in action.

From Fig. 3 here you can see how to jump. I must pull at the opponent's right arm (with which he is pulling me), and push his left chest with my right hand; in this way I neutralize his arm action.

My body must twist to the left to present my right side to him, and I double up my right leg. His left leg, in its sweep at Uchimata or Hanegoshi, is almost sure to hit my right leg somewhere, and so it helps to carry me up in the air. At this point the opponent probably feels that the throw is coming off; but as I am pulling my left arm out and pressing him back with my right, his hips stick and he cannot quite get me down in front of him.

So he tries to recover by getting his raised leg and hip down, but if I have managed things skilfully my left hand pull will hold him in position while I slip down in front of him (Fig. 4). Then I can bring off the throw as in Fig. 5.

FIG. I

FIG. 2

FIG 3

FIG. 4

FIG. 5

The technique is a very risky one while you are still practising it. If you're even a little out in the timing you get caught, because by your jump you help the other man to get you up, and if you cannot maintain yourself in the air until his throwing effort has exhausted itself, it will be a very spectacular throw. Still, a keen student can master the timing, and then it is one of the most fascinating techniques in Judo.

To get good at this trick you must be prepared to be thrown again and again before you get it right; but this is quite a good training for an aspiring Judo student. If you are afraid of failures you never make progress at anything. I recommend keen students to go in for this dashing kind of Judo, because it will give them a great insight into the possibilities of Judo movement and tactics.

15. Two Counters

I. – This set illustrates a pretty counter which can often come off if you are determined enough to go for it. It depends on stepping over the Taiotoshi, which is the commonest escape. Many Judo students do not know what to try when they have jumped over, but stand passively while their opponent recovers.

The essence of the thing is to make your jump and immediately go into a spin on your foot, continuing to pull your opponent so that his body goes on turning in the throwing action, but without your body to throw. This means that you must have anticipated the throw to some extent (not too difficult in the case of many Taiotoshis) and got over before your opponent's throwing action really begins. Now you have an example of 'harmony', as it was technically called in the old knightly arts including Ju-jutsu and fencing. Your opponent is exerting force in a certain direction but you manage to evade it, and then you also exert force in the same direction on your opponent's body, so that both of you are driving along the same line. Your opponent's force not merely meets no resistance but is supplemented by yours. Consequently your opponent loses balance abruptly and without any chance of recovery.

Fig. 3 shows clearly how the pull is continued by using the right arm. A technical detail is that here the final Hiza-guruma is made by pressing rather down on opponent's knee; the variation is indicated because the knee is already rather bent from the Taiotoshi action. It makes the throw somewhat smaller, but also more sure. In contest you must be prepared to drop on the opponent for Newaza if a full point is not given.

This kind of mobile defence and counter is strongly recommended to all Judo students for serious study in practice. By going in bravely for this jump and twist you will learn more about Judo dynamics than from months of static Uchikomi repetition.

FIG. I   FIG 2   FIG. 3   FIG 4

II. – An allied counter, shown in Figs. 1–4 (below), is when the opponent is pulling more down so that there is not the big turning action that gives the opening for Hiza-guruma. In this case you can try taking his leg from the rear as in Fig. 3. Sometimes all you can do is to upset him and drop down for ground-work, but occasionally in contest by some happy accident the timing comes just right and you make your sweep just as he pulls his right leg in towards his left. Then the throw can turn out very well and he will come right off the ground.

FIG I   FIG. 2

FIG. 3   FIG. 4

Many Judo students believe that there is no real counter to Taiotoshi, because the thrower is too low and has both his feet on the ground. However, if you are clever with your feet and can manage to keep your balance in the jump over, you should manage to bring off one of these counters a fair number of times. Even to get near them has the advantage that it makes the opponent nervous about going whole-heartedly in for Taiotoshi. If your attempt at counter has only this result of inhibiting his attacks, it has proved its value to you. As your opponent becomes cautious in his attacks you get correspondingly more possibilities, because you can move more freely yourself. This is one of the important functions of a knowledge of counters.

16. The 'Y'

This shows in diagrammatic form the art of combining two techniques. The whole idea is to come in for both of them in exactly the same way, up to as late a moment as possible. Here you see the entry in Figs. 1–4 on page 56 can lead either on to the straight Taiotoshi, or else an unexpected turn into Ouchigari. The point is to practise coming in for your Ouchi, in repetition and other practice, *in this way.* Then you keep your opponent guessing up to the last moment. It may seem elaborate to keep turning your head away from the opponent even when you mean to try a direct Ouchi, but the whole thing is to make it impossible for him to tell whether you intend an Ouchi at all.

If you don't turn your head away, as in the line 13–14, you give the show away at an early stage. He knows then that when your head is turned towards him it's always Ouchi, and when it's turned away then it's going to be Taiotoshi. In this way you announce to your opponent exactly what you intend.

Keep the stem of the 'Y' as *long* as possible; the sooner the branches diverge, the easier it is for your opponent.

Of course this is not the only method of entry which conceals your ultimate intentions. You can try running at your opponent with your face towards him until the last moment, and then whirling round into a Taiotoshi, or else, as a double-bluff, just keeping on for Ouchi.

But the strategy is to be sure that your pair of throws have the same method of entry, or the same methods of entry. It is quite difficult not to give the game away by making some early differentiation; because *you* know which you intend to do, you unconsciously convey it to your opponent.

One way is to practise Uchikomi of the throws alternately: first Ouchi, then Taiotoshi, then Ouchi again, then Taiotoshi again. Try to get your feet and hand-pull the same for both. Then, when you have got a fair rhythm up, let your body try either one just as it feels. At first you may find it difficult to let yourself go, but the fact is that if you have practised enough, the movements will begin to take place of themselves. This is a high level of Judo technique, but there is no reason why those in the Kyu grades should not have an idea of it and try it out sometimes.

In the end the Judo movements should come as naturally to you as a sneeze when your nose is tickled. In the old classics of the knightly arts all sorts of examples are given; one of them is that even when a man is half asleep if a fly crawls over his face he at once puts out a hand and brushes it away, accurately

but without any thought or effort of will needed. A response as immediate and natural is the aim of the expert in Judo and also in Kendo and the other allied arts.

The point cannot be gone into too much here, but it forms a very interesting field of study, and one which is a great help in activities outside the Judo field.

FIG I

FIG. 2

FIG. 3

FIG. 4

FIG. 5

FIG. 6

17. Renraku-waza: Ouchi into Taiotoshi

There is a close connection between Ouchigari and Taiotoshi, as I have several times emphasized. Now in this sequence you can see one example of the connection. In Figs. 1–3 I am coming in in the Ouchi way – that is to say, I take advantage of the fact that my opponent has his left foot advanced and a trifle out. As I plant my right foot (on the apex of a triangle of which my opponent's feet are the base points), I pull with the left hand just as I should do in Ouchi. I swing my left foot in (see Fig 2) pivoting on the right foot, and in Fig. 3 I am making a sort of Ouchi attack. I say 'sort of' because, in fact, *in this particular case* from the very beginning I am aiming at Taiotoshi, and my Ouchi move is not really an attack but more of a feint. I do, however, make contact with his left leg, and I rely on his reactions to send that leg abruptly back.

(Note here that a beginner will probably not react at all – but in that case he is easy to throw with a genuine Ouchi.)

In Fig. 4 my opponent has sharply withdrawn his left foot, and also shifted his weight a little to the right as a precaution against my threat of the throw to the rear. My right foot comes to the ground, but I am hanging my weight largely on him and not supporting it with this foot. If I am successful, the weight of both of us comes momentarily all on to his right foot, and momentarily he will not be able to move it.

My right hand exercises very little force – beginners tend to put too much force into the right hand at this point in their eagerness to get on with the throw. But it means that their right shoulder becomes stiff and they cannot execute the turn. My right hand just clings on to the opponent and no more, at this stage.

The pull with my left arm is important. The hand turns so that the little finger is uppermost, and the elbow goes naturally upward, as you can see in the picture. I feel all the force is on the little-finger edge, up to the elbow, and down the left side. If I get the action right, he will be pulled smoothy forward. My head is still in the Ouchi position, that is, looking at his body.

In Fig. 5 the throw is about to be executed. The aim is to throw the opponent forward on to a point about 3 ft. in front of me. My head turns abruptly to look at that point, and my hands pull strongly towards it. My legs make a springing up action, to take him in a big trajectory towards the same place.

In Fig. 6 you can see how the right leg is used to lever up the opponent's right shin. If you compare with Fig. 5, you will see how my right leg has been stretched almost straight; this brings it up with great power under his leg and throws him over. This last springing action with the right leg is not absolutely essential to the throw; some experts leave the right leg simply as the fulcrum and bring opponent's body over it. But I have found the springing up action, as shown in these and many other pictures of the present book, most effective if it can be achieved.

18. A Feeble Ouchi

This series illustrates one of the commonest faults in Ouchi – namely that you stay balanced on your rear foot and cautiously peck away at one of the opponent's legs with your other one. (Some people viciously kick, but there is no extra result, except on the opponent's temper.) I do not say that the throw can never come off in this style: it can. But you have to be either very much faster and better balanced than your opponent, or else a lot bigger.

If you try it against a bigger opponent who is anything like your own fighting ability, he will simply sweep your legs away, as in Figs. 4 and 5 here. He can do this because you have not thrown your weight on to him and so he can just stand undisturbed and bring his extra weight into play.

If you are the stand-away-and-peck type, as a cure you might try this jumping Ouchi shown in Fig. 6. It won't come off very much, but it will give you the idea of throwing yourself in. You can nearly always stagger him a little when you get somewhere near it, and that can be a good lead-in for Taiotoshi or some other throw to the front.

FIG. I

FIG. 2

FIG. 3

FIG 4

FIG 5

FIG. 6

19. Throwing the Weight in Ouchigari

In both Taiotoshi and Ouchigari you have to be able to throw the weight, in one case towards your opponent and in one case away. This is a natural pair of throws, and if you compare this section with the section on throwing the weight in Taiotoshi you can see how it is a question of rocking the opponent back and forth with the pair of throws. With one you push with your weight, and with the other you pull. If you can bewilder your opponent so that he doesn't know which one is coming next, you will often get him to lean the wrong way, so that he will be throwing his weight in the same direction as you are throwing your weight. That's when the throw comes off with spectacular effect!

Now suppose you wanted to push hard at something – say to push it over. If you stand very close to it, as in Fig. 1 on page 64, then you find you have got very little thrust. If you wanted to *lift* it then you would be well advised to get as close as possible, but when it is a question of push it is not good to be too near.

Now consider Fig. 2, where the man is well away. There is a very strong push, with most of his weight behind it as the expression has it. But you can see that the push will necessarily be a short one – if the pillar moved back a few inches he would fall on to the floor. So that if you are very far away, you have difficulty in keeping up your push.

Fig. 3 gives about the right distance for a man of medium build – about 2 ft. away from the base of the pillar. This is roughly the position for an Ouchi, and the picture gives the clue to the action of the throw. The weight

FIG. I

FIG. 2

FIG. 3

FIG. 4   FIG. 5

is thrown forward on to the opponent; you must not try to stand on one leg safe and secure and throw him with the other one. The throw is a *push,* and a push with your weight well behind it. Generally, beginners are much too nervous to throw themselves forward at the opponent; you can help yourself to get the idea by practising against a wall like this, until you feel how to rest your weight, and finally throw your weight, against the wall.

For a good contest throw you must go right down to the ground with the opponent; if you don't, he can generally manage to twist out of the full point. But beginners need not go down violently with each other. If the beginner simply rests his weight on the opponent as he throws, he will recover his balance as the opponent goes down and can remain comfortably standing. Figs. 4 and 5 are contest-style throws to be studied by Black Belts.

FIG. 1   FIG. 2   FIG. 3

FIG. 4   FIG. 5   FIG. 6   FIG. 7

FIG. 8   FIG. 9   FIG. 10   FIG. 11

FIG. 12   FIG. 13   FIG. 14   FIG. 15

20. Ouchigari–Taiotoshi Rally

I am coming in **straight** for the Ouchi and then the Taiotoshi. A **circling** action will work for certain opponents, and every Taiotoshi student must be expert in it because there are many people who find it awkward to walk round in a circle; and so if you are skilful in getting them into a circling action, the Taiotoshi often comes off extremely well. But there are others whom you cannot get to move like that, and against them you need to get attacks going to the front and back. This kind of 'straight' attack is particularly necessary against heavy opponents who keep rather static.

When you do the practice of alternating Ouchi and Taiotoshi, try to keep on the same line. Start on one of the lines of the mats and go straight forward along it for your Ouchigari, and keep right on to the end with the Taiotoshi on the same line. At the end your opponent will jump over your Taiotoshi and end up facing the other way; then you chase your opponent back along the same line.

I begin this facing the opponent in a certain position – level Shizentai or right Shizentai. Whichever it is, it is my customary posture from which I launch either Taiotoshi or Ouchigari, and it is *important that both of them should come from the same starting position*. If I have one starting position for Taiotoshi and a different one for Ouchi, I might as well be hoisting a flag to tell the opponent which I mean to do. This point has been discussed before, but I want to mention it again for serious consideration, as it is extremely important in this alternating practice.

I begin with my starting position and try my Ouchigari coming straight at the opponent. The opponent escapes by lifting his leg, and as he does so *I momentarily resume the starting posture* just for an instant (though this time I am closer to the opponent, who is still recovering his balance from the Ouchi attack) before launching into the Taiotoshi. My method of entry for the Taiotoshi should be similar to that for Ouchi. This point too has been explained, but it must be repeated here.

Begin the practice from as far away as possible, because you will have to face large distances against experienced contest opponents and you must be able to throw yourself across them.

My feeling in this practice is that I am rolling a ball at the opponent, the ball being my body. It bounces against him and he goes back away from it. Then I roll it at him again. It may sound strange to give this sort of illustration, but sometimes this kind of vivid image gets people moving in the spirit of the technique much better than detailed explanations in terms of mechanics. And that is the important thing. It is no use merely having an idea in your brain; you have to get the feeling of it in your body action.

21. Kosoto into Taiotoshi

Here the same attacking sequence is shown twice on pages 70-71 – once performed against a taller, and once against a smaller opponent. You can see how very differently the throw is brought off, and this will give some idea of the richness you can find in Judo, if you study.

I. – *Against a Taller Opponent*

Here the attacker, being smaller, has to make use of his advantage, which is greater mobility. Just as the lion in fighting an elephant uses his speed and mobility, and does not attempt a pushing match, so when you are out-weighted you must go in for lightning change of attack and direction.

When I try this Kosotogari as a lead into Taiotoshi, I do not cling to the opponent's foot, but make just the one hooking action. (When Kosoto is tried on its own, you often hang on to the opponent's foot and make two or three attempts.) If I have judged my opponent rightly, he will whip his foot nervously out of the way. When it is in the air he is momentarily, so to say, one legged, and then I have my chance.

I drop my hooking foot on to the ground for an instant, somewhere in front of him, and draw up the other foot towards it or round behind it. In the same breath almost I move into the Taiotoshi. I have to get into position before he can lower his attacked foot so it is a very quick action. A good deal depends on how much I have been able to surprise him, and this is a general principle of a small student's Judo. It does not necessarily follow that I must know a tremendous number of such tricks if I am on the light side; even with say four, I can ring the changes on a number of alternatives and catch the opponent out regularly. All the same a small student should reckon to learn a new one at least every year; once his Judo gets stagnant he has no chance.

FIG I

FIG. 2

FIG 3

FIG. 4

FIG. 1

FIG. 2

FIG. 3

FIG. 4

FIG. 5

FIG. 6

71

II. – *Against a Shorter Opponent*

These pictures show on page 71 the sequence from Kosoto into Taiotoshi demonstrated by Mr. T. Kawamura (7th Dan), who perfected this sequence as a Tokui-waza.

In the first picture, the opponent stands rather away, as he will always tend to do against an opponent with long legs. In the second picture the taller man manages to cover the ground and in the third picture he achieves the attacking position for Kosotogari. Notice particularly the action of the attacker's left arm; he lifts opponent's elbow higher and higher in order to bend him over to the left.

Fig. 4 is the crucial picture. The attacker has a fairly good position for Kosoto, but the defender has been anticipating it and has kept enough suppleness in his body to be able to get the right foot back. He has enough weight on this foot to save himself from being unbalanced over to his left back corner, in spite of the fact that his right elbow has been carried up.

In Fig. 5 he completes his escape by whipping the left foot back out of the hooking action of Kosoto, and forcing his right elbow down. Tori now changes his lifting action into a sudden pull down with the left hand, and if he has managed to get the timing right, he and the opponent are moving the latter's body in the same direction – namely to its right side. Tori is ready to carry his right leg across for the Taiotoshi.

Fig. 6 shows the Taiotoshi, directly to opponent's side. The throw directly to the side requires perfect manoeuvring. Here it comes off because the opponent was made to react strongly in that direction. The throw is made from a distance, the tall man using his advantage (long legs) to the maximum effect. A short man could not expect to bring off this kind of Taiotoshi, but the main interest of Judo in the higher stages is to work out the methods that are particularly suited to one's physique and special advantages, at the same time making the most of opponent's special disadvantages.

Note that in this Taiotoshi the thrower's head has not fallen away to the side, and that his weight is a good deal on the right foot. See page 76 for this type of throw in the stress of contest.

22. Contest Pictures

This picture is a famous Taiotoshi executed by Mr. Daigo (then 6th Dan) against Mr. Natsui (then 5th Dan) in the semi-finals of the All-Japan Judo Championships in 1954. Both the contestants are big men and both became All-Japan Champions. The Taiotoshi has been brilliantly successful; both opponent's feet have come right off the ground, and this means that the thrower got right under and then sprang up from below. Mr. Daigo, though a big man, is noted for the excellence and dexterity of his Judo techniques.

The thrower's centre of gravity is about midway between his two feet which is where it should be for Taiotoshi; the left foot is planted firmly on the ground, the toes pointing well out. The right foot is on the toes, but still takes a good deal of the weight. The head looks down near the left foot.

The left hand must have pulled right out and down, and now as the thrower's body springs up, the hand pinned against it is rising too. This makes the big twist on the opponent's body which whirls him over so completely.

Mr. Natsui has tried to defend by bending the right knee; sometimes the full point can be prevented by getting that knee to the ground before the body lands, so taking some of the impetus out of the throw. However, he has evidently been taken over very quickly, and his head has been brought so far down that the defence cannot succeed.

It is an interesting coincidence that the final of the All-Japan Championship in 1956, two years later, was decided by a Taiotoshi, executed this time by Mr. Natsui on Mr. Daigo. Here it is.

The hip is rather into the opponent, but still it is classed as a Taiotoshi because most of the work is done by the hands – there is no strong hip action against the opponent's body. This is, however, not nearly so 'classical' a throw as the preceding one.

Mr. Daigo, in fact, cleverly succeeded in stepping over the right leg – you can see his foot on tiptoe just beyond. But he was caught in the strong pull and could not manage to save his balance. Mr. Natsui's right foot came off the ground as he twisted his body even more; there is not so much lift in this throw as pull forward and down to the ground. Nevertheless, the opponent was thrown completely, the reason being that his head and shoulders were so well carried over and down.

From the fact that Taiotoshi decided these two contests at the top levels of the All-Japan Championships one can see its importance as a contest technique.

This picture and the last are by courtesy of the Asahi Press.

This Taiotoshi was executed by Mr. Hashimoto (now 7th Dan) teacher at Tenri University. The opponent's left lapel was rather loose, but this makes the right-hand lifting action in the throw stand out clearly. The left hand here is holding at the armpit, which is not the most favourable hold for Taiotoshi, but the effectiveness of the right hand compensates.

If you look carefully you will see that the opponent is standing entirely on the right foot – you can just see his left foot in the air behind the right one. To secure this position is one of the important manoeuvres for a Taiotoshi man.

It is likely that the opponent was standing in a left Shizentai position momentarily, and then Mr. Hashimoto made a fast attack with Kosotogari against the advanced left foot, making the opponent withdraw it hurriedly. Then, without moving his own supporting foot (the left), the attacker shot straight across into the Taiotoshi, getting a big lift from the right hand at the same time. Not moving the left foot will have the disadvantage that it leaves his feet rather far apart, but against that he has got in so fast that his opponent is still on one leg – and so the throw comes off. (For this sequence compare Kosoto– Taiotoshi, pages 71-72.)

Note the thrower's chin well down on his left chest.

Fighting to get the left hand in; on the right on page 77 is Mr. Inokuma, twice All-Japan Champion. His opponent Mr. Koga (5th Dan) is passing the lapel over to get hold with the left hand. (See pages 46-47 and also below.)

FIG. 1

FIG. 2

FIG. 3

FIG. 4

The pull is extremely good, but the opponent has managed to bring his left foot well in and is raising the right foot to jump over the Taiotoshi when it comes. Everything will now depend on whether the thrower can keep up the pull and retain enough balance and mobility to make two or three tries at the Taiotoshi; if he can he brings it off in most cases. The opponent finds it increasingly difficult to keep stepping over the Taiotoshi; in the contest picture on page

75, Mr. Daigo, in spite of having got his foot over, was still thrown by the strong pull.

A very satisfactorily executed Taiotoshi from an All-Japan Championship. The' opponent has been brought completely on to the left front of his supporting foot, and is on one leg. The pull has been such as to take his head and shoulders right down, and the thrower's attacking leg (the left) fitted well round the attacked leg. You can see how the thrower has sprung up from underneath, and that the opponent is being thrown to his left front corner and not directly to the front. This makes it very difficult for him to execute the jump over the throw.

Note that the thrower's weight is well forward out to the left, and there is no danger of his losing balance and falling backwards – the great fault in Taiotoshi.

The thrower here has fallen back – his weight is mostly on his left (supporting leg). As a result his pull is completely broken up, and the opponent has, in fact, succeeded in getting over the throw with both his feet.

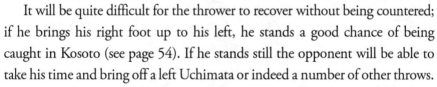

It will be quite difficult for the thrower to recover without being countered; if he brings his right foot up to his left, he stands a good chance of being caught in Kosoto (see page 54). If he stands still the opponent will be able to take his time and bring off a left Uchimata or indeed a number of other throws.

The opponent seems to have kept his balance very skilfully, although the pull looks as if it was a strong one and the attacker has certainly carried his body into it. The only poor point is that the head has not been turned, and this may be one reason that it did not come off.

But, when all is said, even a very fine movement will not succeed if the opponent can foresee it and adapt his balance and posture in time.

A very tall man's Taiotoshi, by T. Leggett. The distribution of the weight is correct, though the right leg is rather straight, and the opponent has been well brought round. The latter was Mr. T. Daigo, then All-Japan Champion, and in fact though he looks gone he has skilfully managed to cross the attacking leg enough to reserve sufficient balance to save the throw. This was in an exhibition.

Inokuma v. Kaminaga—both have been all-Japan Champions.

The crucial moment! The attacker on the left has made an opening Ouchi, and the man on the right has whipped his left leg up to avoid it.

Both men are momentarily right off the ground. There are opportunities on both sides, but it is just at this point that many Judo pairs declare a sort of mutual armistice; they both stay where they are and settle down to a normal safe posture.

It is true it is quite an unstable position to be in, but the whole thing is that the opponent too is floating in the air in a splendid position to be thrown. It is a question of courage and 'dash', and all aspiring young Judo students should practise throwing themselves boldly in on these occasions. It is 'first in gets it!' If you exercise yourself in getting in from such seemingly unfavourable situations, you will learn how to balance yourself all the time. Then you will be able to get your opponent rattled quite easily; the ordinary Judo student feels completely lost when outside the little range of positions which they know the feel of.

Note that here both sides have chances. The opponent has not merely survived the Ouchi but has kept his left hip supple and drawn the leg clear. This is a good example of keen Judo, and this kind of contest is the best and most instructive.

CHAMPIONSHIP JUDO

CPSIA information can be obtained
at www.ICGtesting.com
Printed in the USA
BVHW031954190822
645019BV00012B/354

9 781911 467113